MAXed OUT

OUT

Portland Transit Poems

Poems

||||||||||||||||||||||||||||||||||||||

Rick McMonagle

||||\\\\||||\\\\|||

KAREN,

Writing together
to Eternity!

MAXed OUT

Portland Transit Poems

Contents

Acknowledgments

Robin Moore, cabinmate, author, storyteller, publisher, teacher, for motivating and inspiring me to get my writing published, and for lifelong encouragement.

Jennifer and Mark, keepers of Luna House in Oceanside, Oregon, for letting me stay in their ample cottage with a true rock wall out the window, which gave me some quiet coastal time to write.

David Jenkins, for following my dreams, pulling me out of the whirlpools, and guiding me to the other shore.

Olivia and Zoe for brown-eyed wonder.

Jane Lincoln Taylor, for her editorial inspiration, insights and punctual expertise.

Portland, for creating a friendly and affordable transportation system where even the drivers crack jokes over the public-address system for sleepy-eyed commuters.

My fellow MAX passengers. Your presence, appearance, humor, compassion, aggression, conversations, irritations, insanity, moods, and manners made these poems possible. Deep gratitude to you. Equally Ready, Equally Aboard, Equally Reaching Our Destinations.

Introduction

I began writing these poems in the fall of 2017 after starting a new job in downtown Portland, Oregon. I usually take the MAX train to work. The Metropolitan Area Express (MAX) is a three county, color-coded rail transportation system serving the Portland area and operated by TriMet. Orange is my MAX line and it takes about twenty minutes on a good day to reach my destination. The cars are often packed with Clack County residents, Reedites, the medical herd heading toward OHSU, PSU students, city bureaucrats, and a mix of others like me. I quickly realized that this diverse array of humanity, with its moods and behaviors, was waiting for me to witness and record in my small black unlined notebook with a ballpoint pen. It was my commuting Garden of Earthly Delights.

The banquet kept unfolding, revealing itself, ride after ride, stop after stop, who came in, who went out. I could not help writing down what I saw, heard, smelled, felt, and imagined. It seemed the mornings were more bountiful than the afternoons—but not always. I wonder if you'll be able to tell what time of day a specific poem was written?

And then there was the outside—morphing tag posts, gazing goddess murals, trickster crows and purposeful gulls, zipping bikes, homeless compounds, and railroad crossing stuck cars. I saw it all.

I sure got my money's worth! A ticket to ride revealed a kaleidoscopic universe of committed commuters peppered with Portlandia possibilities. Please hold on....

Ross Island Bridge Blue—The Cover

The bluesque color of the cover was selected to match the newly painted "unusually unbureaucratic hue" of the Ross Island Bridge that's featured in the poem, "Lady Day Bridge." I was impressed by the color selection as it seemed rich, beyond blue and the typical dullish finish of most civic metal projects.

First, a little history according to Wikipedia: *The bridge's girders were originally painted black, but in 1955–56 they were repainted green. In 1961, Portland architect Lewis Crutcher suggested repainting all of Portland's downtown-area bridges from black into different colors, and the proposal also included changing the Ross Island Bridge's color to blue. The proposal was approved by the Multnomah County Commission, and repainting of the Ross Island Bridge was carried out in the summer of 1965. The bridge's color remains blue today, specifically "phthalo blue."*

I wrote the folks at the Oregon Department of Transportation (ODOT) because they own the bridge and managed the re-painting project. They were timely and responsive to my request to learn the exact bluish finish color of the bridge. In one of its public statements about the color, ODOT said, *"Five coats of paint will be applied to the Ross Island Bridge with the last coat a deep blue-green, the color it was last painted in 1967. Faded remnants of the 1967 paint job can be seen in places on the bridge."* And, in a reply to my email, *"That paint color at the time was called phthalo blue and green. The paint for the recent painting of the bridge was called 'Ross Island Original' and number was Wasser W21.4019."*

I contacted The Wasser Corporation in Auburn, Washington for a sample so I could try to match it for the cover. Soon after I sent my request, I received an envelope in the mail with a swatch of the color with the following identifier:

WASSER
W21.4019
MC-LUSTER 2.8 ROSS ISLAND
BRIDGE
GLOSS (70-75)

We tried to match this magnificent hue, "like all the Portland tattoo ink mixed together," for the cover of MAXed OUT from the available color selections.

Rick

The doors are closing

Train departing

Please hold on

MAX

Metropolitan Area Express
5 LINES
Red Orange Green Yellow Blue
97 Stations
60 Miles Long
Standard-Gauge Track
(1,435 mm)
145 Cars
Over 116k Weekday Boardings
EQUALS
40 Million Annual
Boardings
825
VOLTS

First Monday

Almost red ripe
Strawberry hue dawn
Parallel stanza sky stripes
Half note of a Moon
Directing our off-key
Monday yawn
This 70-degree-to-be
First full Daylight Savings
Workday 2018.
Spring jacket found
In back of bedroom closet,
Lightweight, fits well,
Zips work,
To ventilate feelings
Of another season ending
And new ones vaping in.

State of Wonder

"Daddy, look
  at that gorgeous
  Sunset!
  Honey, it's a
  Sunrise.
  Daddy, look
  at that handsome
  Sunrise!"

Orange Line Blues

No one
  singing
  or
  busking
Like the boy
  on the bus
  between Athens
  and the Port of Piraeus
Excruciating
  to all
  except
  me.
As I got off
  I handed him
  ancient Greek coins
To the regret
  of the full house.

New Year

More paper
Lap books
Today
Than
Electronics,
Holiday gifts?
Determined to be
Most
Read City—
Move over Moline,
Minneapolis, Munich.

Book Battle of the Sexes

Her head moves
back and forth
trying to keep up
with its volleying eyeballs
following the game
of words
on the page
of her clay court transit book
royalty jousting tennis match
between Queen Billie Jean King
& Bobby the Court Jester Riggs

Twenty Minute Infatuation

We'll never stare
at each other again.
It's just these few
minutes of flame,
pedestalling each other
onto the White Stag billboard,
surging down the Willamette
hand-in-hand
surfing centurion sturgeons.
There is no other
in this minute slice
of space & time,
not even minor role
momentary walk-ons.
Never the one that blew in
the open doors
at the Grand Mosque
Metro stop,
Gaudi's serpentine promenades,
Louvre lover's light,
A touch of Mediterranean,
LaLaLosTehrangeles.
Poof!
One of us vanishes first,
as we must,
not even
never more,
Amore.

Shapes

All three
same full body
type,
like attracts
like the movie review
one of them gives
of *The Shape of Water*,
Oscar winner last night.
"I saw it yesterday.
Not the type of movie
I usually watch.
Heartwarming love story.
Weird."
She grows gills
just like him,
aqueous shape-shifter,
to meet in the end
under the full
rapture of the sea.

Believe It

"I'm
  Unblowoffable.
  Believe
  It!"

Winter Wear

He wields
Finisher T-shirt
& shorts.
Das Winter!
Carburetor belly
burns
beans, buns, brews
All
the livelong
Ride.

Undercover

She exits
one stop early.
I know,
she works in my building.
Met by two guys
bearing gold metal badges
but not in any obvious uniform.
    They all know
    and talk about it.
She usually doesn't wear socks
even on cold days,
but today brandishes knee high
black leather boots,
thick Stephen King novel
staring out from heavy
shoulder bag.

New Moon Morning

New moon sickle
slung between black wires
its live arc could take down
the City
but in my viewscape
it stays Cool
up there beaming.

Crows play chicken with the cars
and arouse our morning stupor,
while gulls gallop wing
towards delicious dump delicacies
somewhere east of here.

The scaffold trolley line
construction above O.M.S.I.*
now revealed —
electro Tower of Babel
beaming archaic apocalyptic
algorithmic projections
to the Black Submarine
docked in the murky river,
from the *Outer Mystery Secret Institute.

Taking Off The Gloves

"Nope,
  Portlanders for the most part
  don't wear gloves in the winter.
  Not sure if it's a coolness thing or what.
  But what gripes me is they don't put
  mittens on their kids even
  in open, windblown strollers!
  Fingercicles for sure!
  Don't they know about Midwestern mitten clips
  that grip onto the end of a coat sleeve,
  or the old-fashioned long piece of yarn
  tied to each mitten and wound through
  one coat sleeve,
  around the neck and down
  the other sleeve?
  Never lose those!"

Life and Death

Ephemeral glow of Mt. Hood,
Our Mountain Our Pole Star,
Pouring amber sun shock
into the Orange Line over
the river this unusually clear
winter morning.
No other lifting our hearts
from low elevation screens,
the same day a climber
fell one thousand feet to his death
after summiting and reveling
in that glacial glory.
Can we see the solar glint
off the rescue helicopter
dispatched from the balmy coast,
the crew risking life and limb
for one climber
this radiant day?

Bloodlines

"I'm like his dad,
  His BIOLOGICAL DAD!
  I took off my hat
  & sunglasses.
  He had on like
  this black duster."

Doctor Golden

My real Doc sits across the aisle,
unbelievable at morning
MAX rush hour,
crisp charcoal casual pants
with matching running shoes.
He doesn't notice me
in his obsessive phone focused tapping
while white-ear-budded
listening to the *New England Journal of Medicine*
podcast about the perils
of cell phone radiation.
On task
like in the office
like no other on the train
has seen me in my clean briefs perched
on the edge of the stainless exam table
wondering if this will be the one
after listening to my lungs
when he says it's incurable,
six months to live.
He departs ahead of schedule
and I feel his glimpse
as he passes
but what do you say
to your terminal patient
in public—

How's the tumor?
I can't believe you're going to work
with only a few months left to live!
Are you an organ donor?
Have you planned your last meal?
Any dreams still left in the bucket?
Did you put me in your will?
What a gloomy dark day, eh?
It was nice knowing ya!

Reflexology

"I take
  a picture
  every year
  of my feet
  to see how
  they've
  developed."

Maximus Olympus

Interior grey vinyl bellows
disguise inner workings
of the coupling mechanisms
that bind us and the cars together
while circle floor joints swirl like
a metropolitan discus
spins whoever is on it
forcing your balance
and continual moving views
of the City in Lights
like a Spandex fitness machine
pumping early morning workout.

Look out!

Act weird!
You may be next!
In print!
O Super Natural Portlandia!

MAX Buffoonery

Business casual guy
becomes Mr. Buffoon,
at least his shoes,
by the sideshow circus reflection
in the closed glass door distortion
aka long clown shoes.
Does anyone else see this?
Does this happen to everyone,
or just on the day
you make your pitch
for a long overdue raise?

Two Dog Wild Ride

Wild ride on the train home from work today. I find a
seat across the aisle from a large tawny Pit Bull, which for
some reason, maybe to protect my throbbing jugular,
the owner tugs into an open wedge against the window.
Then another guy announces, "Would some of you please
give up your seats to my elderly mother and pregnant
wife"—sure covered all of the bases with that one. I get
up and move back and hold onto the yellow metal pole
by the door. Then another guy careens onto the next pole
and starts trashing talking the Pit. "Why doesn't someone
put that Pit in front of the train and run over it, the driver
wouldn't care, who would, fuckin Pits?" Then another
canine caretaker gets up and pushes the orange Call Driv-
er button and says, "Hey, there's a drunk here harassing
my service dog"—a thick Siberian Husky. The driver says,
"Where are you?" She says, "In the back of the train." The
drunk woman weaves toward the front of the train grum-
bling. I didn't see her do anything to the dog, but maybe
she was beaming high-frequency freak waves. Then the
drunk starts imitating a loud woman on a phone when
she hears exciting words like "love" and "interesting" and
yells LOOOOVVVVEEEE!!! and laughs loud and INTER-
ESTING??!!! And we all look at each other and some smile
and wonder what's next. Then for some reason, the lady
with the Husky pushes the Call Driver button again and

tells him the drunk is at it again, but the drunk isn't even visible, so maybe she registers canine brain beeps or the drunk has one of those silent-to-humans high pitched dog whistles or an AKC app on her imaginary phone, and the driver says, "At the next stop," which is right then, and a fluorescent green TRIMET security worker comes on, calmly says, "Where is she?" Finds her, escorts her out onto the cold wet platform, the doors close, we start moving, and as we pass the drunk gives an emphatic middle-finger salute to us all.

TRIMET RESPECTS (~~CIVIL~~) DRIVEL RIGHTS

ALL YE, ALL YE, ALL YE, HAVE THE GOD AWFUL
RIGHTS TO PROCLAIM

no sense, nonsense, twaddle, claptrap,
balderdash, gibberish, rubbish,
mumbo jumbo, garbage,
informal poppycock, piffle,
tripe, bull, hogwash, babble, baloney,
codswallop, flapdoodle, jive, guff,
bushwa, tommyrot, bunkum,
vulgarity, slang, crapola,
verbal diarrhea,
blather, ramble, gibber, prattle,
gabble, waffle,
let saliva or mucus flow
from the mouth or nose,
dribble and chatter

Primal

He walks up to the stop
in an over-the-top pink coat
bleached moussed hair
patent leather low-cut black loafers
minus the pennies
lavender button-down business shirt
pressed dark pants
fully opened umbrella
belts a blood curdling
eardrum piercing scream
then calmly and without further ado
steps delicately
onto the newly arrived train.

Seeing Red

"When I first started off
  Everything was RED—
  hat, sleeping bag,
  pants, shirt.
  Everything I owned
  was red!
  It was weird."

Pulp of the Proletariat

If it were dark
the glow of the Capitalist
Materialist screens
would brighten our
pale NW IWW faces.
Almost all plugged in
compared to
Moscow Metro
  reading pulp
    BB-OO-KS
from left to right
Cyrillic literati.

Fingers

woman knitting away
fingers fabulous morning flitting
appropriate cascadia greens and blues
she alone is preserving
low-carbon art
with humane
handcraft
grace

The Footsie Index

When you are lucky enough
to land a seat
you are eyeball-to-eyeball
with every other seated rider
and you can't stare
them in the face
for the entire ride
according to the Transit
Code of Honor,
so downcast gaze drifts
to a Sea of Shoes
of all makes & models—
black brown red blue
orange green yellow
animal vegetable mineral
MAX line matching materials.

Not Guilty

She's reading,
Guilt by Association
by Marcia Clark

Los Angeles D.A. Rachel Knight is a tenacious, wise-cracking,
and fiercely intelligent prosecutor in the city's most elite division.
When her colleague, Jake, is found dead at a grisly crime scene,
Rachel is shaken to the core. She must take over his toughest case:
the assault of a young woman from a prominent family.

For weeks
she's been obvious about this
holding the book up to her face
for all to see
in her sunny lioness socks
as if to protect her Achilles
from novel attacks jumping out
of the pages
or another rabid commuter
but no one would confront her
regally crowned with a corporate
Mohawk cut
high-tech helmet
of cropped circuitry cushioning
her cortex.

Witness

"Twelve jurors can decide
  your fate.
I really don't know
what's going to happen.
They burned down his house
and stole his boat
for the insurance.
They say anything you say
can be held against you,
the difference between 25 years
or Life.
No one on the MAX train
is paying attention
until it's too late.
I was there for those murders.
I saw the tapes.
Everyone yelled Oh! Oh! Oh!
I've been there
and cried
like everyone else."

Fare Check

Three fare enforcers
board the train
in their Big Gold
Badge Bling
and one announces
    "Fare Check!"
Hefty fine if caught
or expired.
Most have the electro-dollars
on their phones
or a Get Out of Jail Free
Card with a silver metallic
magnetic paper valid ticket swatch.
Or not.
And then the fun begins
when the Fairy Cops
puff up
to bust
a fair man
or maiden.

Full Tank

Car packed to the Max,
urban-sardine-cannery.
Driver explains one train
couldn't get out of Park,
cold frost morning,
we didn't want to get out
of Bed either.
My view limited
to the door glass
in my face
and the half moon
playing peekaboo with the fog
pouring over the West Hills.
Train starts slowing
for my downtown stop,
and as I turn toward the door
I see an ivory woman
sitting cross-legged on the grimy floor
in the wide wheelchair section
nursing her long-haired baby
as innocent as can be,
not covered at all &
calm as if on a crowded Oaxacan
chicken bus winding down the mountain
from the California yoga lactation retreat.

Mt. St. Helens

Will you bake
a fluffy snowball
bridal groom cupcake
for the LGBQ-RSTUVWXYZ
wedding?
Or did
your Holy Book
prohibit you
from spewing sugary
celebratory creations
from the volcanic oven
of frosty delights?

Magical Meal

"He's always been
  like a second father to me,
  always asks if I need anything,
  how am I doing.
  We're going over there
  for dinner tonight.
  I'll make something
  from the *Harry Potter Cookbook*."

Late Claus

Permanent
Peppermint Santa
Hops on
Groundhog Day
Red stocking
Hat
Fifty gallon belly
Shopping bag purse
White bread beard
Bright orange coat
420 friendly

Cool Jerk

Train stops as usual
then HARD BRAKE
& we all lunge
in whatever direction
we face.
All of the adults look worried —
    Homeless sleeping suicide bump?
    Terrorist frozen water bottle trick?
But the few little kids remaining
    laugh loud thrill ride
Cool lurch urban buckaroo fun.

Balancing Act

School teacher
grades handwritten
student papers
with a pink-tipped pen
standing in the middle
of the aisle,
no hand holds,
writes margin comments
then a longer note
on the last page
of each.
She always wears a skirt
& hangs her bike.

Service Dog

My "owner" is bent over in pain,
but he's usually that way.
He looks like the kind of dude
who would beat me,
but he's never lifted a paw,
I swear.
He's just super suffering.
Just look at his crazy beast eyes,
every knuckle tattooed,
and check out that exotic bone
bracelet he's wearing—
for the life of me,
I drool every time he wears it!
You can see by how I wrap my metal "leash"
around his legs, back and forth
back and forth, that I don't
like riding on trains,
too noisy, odorous, cramped,
you know—HUMAN!
And that bag of aluminum cans he hauls around,
the clatter drives me canine crazy.
Doesn't he know it sounds like
a train wreck (no pun intended) to me
with every pick up and put down??

So I go over and put my head
on this other dude's knee.
I picked him
because he smelled kind
and didn't have one of those buzzing
gizmos in this hands.
He petted me so sweet, I woulda
went home with him — well not really.
I really love My Dude,
it's just that his appearance makes
other Bros question my sanity.

But, Mrs. Dude is Divine.
I love her to death.
She always scents right.
It's embarrassing, but I can't stop
crotching her and all of that other
lovey-dovey doggie stuff I do.

I get so doggone tired of always wearing
my "Service (whatever that means!) Dog" vest.
It gets too hot in the summer
and it looks like I'm wearing one of those
Dogawful corporate logo shirts.
What a scam!
It gets us into the wildest places,
like the Free Clinic day or night
(can't they let a dog sleep?)
or them "homeless shelters."
Woo, now some of those people just make me quiver,
especially their dogs, like them pouncing Pits,
GGGRRRRR, get them away from me…

Okay, I'm leaving now,
my pack finally found a seat,
and I have to go since Dude
has that wire thing around my metal necklace
and where Dude goes, I go,
But that's okay, maybe that's what "Service"
is all about—putting my front paws
on his shoulder
and nuzzling his neck.

Silver City

Woman sits on her stainless boudoir
bench at the South Waterfront stop,
oblivious to the passing rush of hauling trains
and the OHSU scrub scrum.
Silver nail polished toes
exposed in summery sandals
shimmer in fog droplets
next to a pair
of shiny silver office shoes
and two white cloth balls
which she unfurls
as twin slinky socks
she slides on,
left foot first,
then the magic silver slipper
and then the white orb other
until she has a very voila vision
two heel click to start
her very marvy metallic day.

Stonedhenge

of scatter rock remains
broken circles of the homeless
transitory tent spots,
sleep rookeries
for a night
on the so green cropped
roadway slope,
even try to catch
a goodnight's steep sleep
when the rest of us
are cushioned
in our bolted flat
boarded nests

Today

Our train
Hit a bicyclist
At 4:35 pm now
First responders flashing
One of the doors half opened
Some of us hopping down to the gravel
Look in both directions the boy in plaid shorts
Lies on his back smack dab in middle of the tracks
Knees to the sky medics cleaning & gauzing & taping
We hope in heavy heart of hearts that he'll be holy healed

Dream Train

Driver stops the train
in the middle of Tilikum Crossing.
Comes over the PA:
"I had a dream last night
that I was a muffler.
[Pause]
It was exhaust-ing."
Turns off PA,
resumes trip
over to the west side.

Learning Spanish

The stops and open door
announcements
are BILINGUAL,
Not Tlingit and Tamil,
Greco or German,
but Gringo y Español.
La Chiqua es Ingles
y Los Macho es Matadorish.
I now know my Latino left
from my Latina right,
Izquierda o Derecho.
How Linea el color Naranja
Merges into Amarillo o Verde y
When Roja veers off to El PeDeEx.
The Tokyo touristas
just tap their phones…

Neighbor

Rapido man
writes in a little red notebook
with a blood toned pen
in his left hand
to match his cherry shoes
and tangerine pants—
He's looking at me!
Won't he let me be his poem?

Off the *Wall Street Journal*

He plops in almost wearing
a baby blue toga-like blanket
over his shoulder
and dragging on the ground,
drops absorbent adult diaper pads
on the seat first, then falls
onto it in total intestinal comfort.
He interrogates the innocent
woman across the way:
    Where are all of these people from?
    What are they doing on the train?
    Where's Milwaukie?
    Where's Southwest?
He concludes by revealing
a clear plastic bag tube
and opens today's edition
of the *Wall Street Journal.*

Tall, Dark & Tension

Black crew cut
caps ridge lined face
fully plowed brow
locked the whole ride,
gold wedding band
on the proper finger
for magnetic polar balance
and civic cover.
Ever-present full mouth frown,
inverted smile,
East meets West
facial non-recognition,
listens to yellow Voodoo
Doughnut size headset
the full trip broadcast,
devastated by the Nikkei downfall,
shattered by the Shanghai tumble.
When he stuffs his hands
into his front coat pockets
I peer for pistol profiles
or switch blade bulge
& I'd jump off the train
Calling 911 as I fly,
but none protruding.
He retreats at City Hall
to fight the good fight,
no virtual train car teeth
broke, busted or damaged
on the ride.

Tail Tales

"I am no longer angry
  because of this dog."

"He's not a dog,
  he's human."

"Who said animals
  don't have souls?"

"I always spoil
  my animals."

"He's like a little bear,
  he sleeps with me
  curled up in my arms."

The Devil Book

I thought entering the jammed morning
train was the vicious vector,
but he maintained the wounded way,
tense lips,
onyx no-eye emotion sunglasses,
as he read the demonic text
the complete ticket.
Why would someone do that
to himself and others
right after breakfast
and in the midst of an unfolding
at least half-full day?
What does that spell
for his future,
our incarnations?

The Beast

He rolls backwards
out the door ramp.
Comes back in shrieking
at the auburn-haired
woman who breastfed
her curly-haired toddler on the floor
the other day.
Wheelchair goes back out
squealing, incoherent hollering.
She says very distinctly,
"You are yelling
 at a woman and a child."
He counters with
bitch, spit, middle finger,
hand on crotch,
evil eye venom erupting
to Mother and Child
he shakes to the core.

R-E-S-P-E-C-T

She taps me on the arm,
asks me if I want her seat.
She's one of six close-by
young and able occupying
seats reserved for elderly
& some-abled.
Since I'm neither
though some might disagree
with my sterling hair
and stubble,
I say no thanks,
I enjoy standing,
plus I'm practicing
my tai chi
& will be sitting
most of the day.

Bond, Jane Bond

She must be covert,
TriMet spy T007.
Always gets off
at a different stop.
Or a perpetual early riser,
maybe staycation tourist.
Squeezes in & out
crowded morning commutes
taking auditory notes
and clandestine camera captures
our impressions
for the mandatory monthly
public terror report
of how many would be dead
if another knife wielding wacko
started slashing
because his embedded EyePhone
received a vibrating Spam message.
Jane prefers hers
stirred not shaken.

Lady Day Bridge

Diana Ross Island Bridge
   to Rose Island Bridge
      to Eros (Rose remixed) Island Bridge
is getting a makeover,
painted an underwater earthy blue
like all the Portland tattoo ink
mixed together—
stir it up little darling,
Billie Holiday bluer
than any blue
since—
unusually unbureaucratic hue,
a bridge to everywhere,
Tilikum's face lifted upstream
Playmate.

Green and orange dots,
a scramble of workers,
move along the suspended walkways
like early morning rats
jostling over the river
searching for a morning meal.

Two workers Father and Son,
fell to their injury
early on
some feat to recover
and save them from Unholy Ghosts,
now the red rescue boat
is parked all day
underneath
to retrieve Fallen Angels.

It's a magnormous job
to wash, de-rust, prime & paint
an entire bridge
over the wide Willamette,
Confederate Gray primer first coat,
metal blued to the finish —
the Union wins again!

We watch it primp up
beneath changing light shows
like Lady Day brushing
on black-and-blue mascara,
smudged sweat and tears,
fragile fruit hanging onto
the edge of complete stardom,
over the River of Fears
twinkling all alone
on the cosmic stage
all the other stars
blazing her way.

Tour de Tilikum

Bikes buzz by the disembarking train
in front of Jane's green deli,
Japanese French Romano
Shimano Gitane Campagnolo,
Pedal plebian pedestrian power
Zoom students, execs, teachers,
Bureaucrats, Zen Buddhists,
Brew enthusiasts,
Urban crow wranglers,
Caffeine desperados.

Five-Cent Beers

"Five-cent Beers!
  It was probably Miller
  or something
  like that.
  Hell, I'd drink
  any beer for five cents!"

You're It!

Tagger's
    Code
      of
         Honor
Do Not Touch
The magnificent
Wacky profound
Polychrome murals
Blushing the backsides
Of dozens of track facing
Brick walled and iron easels

Omaha

Pus eye sun.
Grim again morning.
Joni Mitchell's Woodstock
in my head
on my trudge
to the train.
The entire ordeal
is a paved over parking lot.
He's meeting her
from 36 years ago
in Omaha
because it's halfway between
then and now.
A C&W song is being butchered there,
stench of stockyards,
largest platter of bovine flesh
this side of Pluto,
a motel, truckers, dead Winnebagos,
Safeway, Denny's, Starbucks, Shell,
Shock of Aging.
Endings where you left off.

Purple Haze

She emerges voluptuous
from the Royal Coach,
her beyond bodacious lips
Painted a Purple Phase
of Jubilant Ecstasy
to match her telepathic vibrant smile
like every violet fruit that ever existed
at full ripeness alchemized together
to paint her lips
a bougainvilleanic majesty
to match her gold-trimmed
other worldly headdress
worthy of a celestial serenade—
Jimi is rising from the Dead
As is Jerry
And Blind Lemon Jefferson
And Brother Ray Charles
You are the Sunshine of My Life Stevie Wonder,
To lip read lip-to-lip with her,
dancing cheek-to-cheek
ecstatic lip sync.

Magnolia

Flaming magnolia blossoms
light the pallid way
like celestial torches
all-day lights
drawing us away
from the glass citadels
that fall behind.
Magnolia was how the Spanish
post office worker pronounced my name
when an American aerogram arrived
at the tiny Iberian post office
standing in the clump of expats
waiting for homemade news.
That's how I learned
Cousin Honeygirl died of cancer,
Where-At-All-Over.
She always remembered my birthday
with a fancy Joseph Horne
Pittsburgh department store
present, a shirt we could never afford.
She's the eternal flame
pointing beyond the clouds,
illuminating our morning montage.

About the Author

Rick McMonagle was born and raised in Pittsburgh, Pennsylvania. His poetry lineage includes a Calabrian great-uncle, Francesco Capilupi, who fell in love, left the priesthood, emigrated to NYC and wrote poems; John Haag, his first poetry teacher at Penn State and who was a student of Theodore Roethke; and Allen Ginsberg and Anne Waldman at Naropa University where he received a Poetics Certificate. He is the author of three books of poetry: Light Tips, Moorish Journal and Spencer Butte Meditations. He lives and works in Portland, Oregon.

CPSIA information can be obtained
at www.ICGtesting.com
Printed in the USA
FSHW010905040121
77359FS